Expanding Leadership Impact

A Practical Guide To Managing People And Processes

Kevin R. Kehoe

First published in 1994 by Richard Chang Associates, Inc., USA.

This edition published in 1995 by Kogan Page Ltd.

Kogan Page Limited
120 Pentonville Road
London N1 9JN

British Library Cataloguing in Publication Data

A CIP record for this book is available from the British Library.

ISBN 0 7494 1658 0

Printed and bound in Great Britain by
Biddles Ltd, Guildford and King's Lynn

ACKNOWLEDGMENTS

About The Author

Kevin R. Kehoe, owner of Kevin Kehoe & Company, is an experienced executive, consultant, and educator. He is widely known and highly regarded for his leadership development, total quality, and reengineering expertise.

The author would like to acknowledge the support of the entire team of professionals at Richard Chang Associates, Inc. for their contribution to the guidebook development process. In addition, special thanks are extended to the many client organizations who have helped us shape the practical ideas and proven methods shared in this guidebook.

Additional Credits

Editors: Scott Rimmer and Sarah Ortlieb Fraser

Reviewers: P. Keith Kelly and Ruth Larsen

Graphic Layout: Christina Slater

Cover Design: John Odam Design Associates

ACKNOWLEDGMENTS

Preface

The 1990's have already presented individuals and organizations with some very difficult challenges to face and overcome. So who will have the advantage as we move toward the year 2000 and beyond?

The advantage will belong to those with a commitment to continuous learning. Whether on an individual basis or as an entire organization, one key ingredient to building a continuous learning environment is *The Practical Guidebook Collection* brought to you by the Publications Division of Richard Chang Associates, Inc.

After understanding the future *"learning needs"* expressed by our clients and other potential customers, we are pleased to publish *The Practical Guidebook Collection*. These guidebooks are designed to provide you with proven, *"real-world"* tips, tools, and techniques—on a wide range of subjects—that you can apply in the workplace and/or on a personal level immediately.

Once you've had a chance to benefit from *The Practical Guidebook Collection*, please share your feedback with us. We've included a brief *Evaluation and Feedback Form* at the end of the guidebook that you can fax to us.

With your feedback, we can continuously improve the resources we are providing through the Publications Division of Richard Chang Associates, Inc.

Wishing you successful reading,

Richard Y. Chang
President and CEO
Richard Chang Associates, Inc.

Table Of Contents

"To lead is to go before."

—Webster

"To lead the people, walk behind them."

—Lao-tsu

CHAPTER ONE

INTRODUCTION

The preceding quotes provide vastly different views of leadership. Which one do you think is correct? Perhaps they both are. But how can you be both first and last? It's simple: an effective leader stands before and behind his or her people at all times. This duality is an essential element of productive leadership.

Another important element of leadership is preparation. There is an adage that anyone can be a captain on calm seas. And it's true; stormy weather is the real test of leadership. A good captain always knows both the crew's and ship's capabilities, which is critical in times of crisis. Likewise, a good leader knows the capabilities of the people and the organization they lead.

Why Read This Guidebook?

In a dramatically changing business world, leadership science needs to keep pace with technological innovation. Popular management techniques become obsolete almost as soon as they are implemented. So, in today's business climate, success depends on the courage to let go of the old leadership models and implement new ones. Nobody will be able to win today using yesterday's techniques.

This guidebook will help you master a new science of leadership. It provides effective leadership methods that can immediately be put into practice. You will learn how to assess your organization and the processes that drive it. In addition, a practical, real-world leadership model is presented, one that you can adopt or adapt to help navigate your organization through even the stormiest seas.

Who Should Read This Guidebook?

Anyone who is in a leadership role or aspires to be in one can benefit from the information in this guidebook. Whether the scope of your leadership applies to an organization, department, division, committee, quality team, or just a single task, you'll be able to apply the lessons presented in this guidebook.

Ask yourself the following questions:

Are you in charge of a team, running a division or managing a department?
Is your boss asking you to do more with less?
Are you finding that what worked for your boss isn't working for you?
Are leadership responsibilities overwhelming you?
Do you want to take on new leadership roles?
Have you failed to learn anything new about leadership in the past year?

If you answered yes to any of these questions, then you need to expand your leadership impact.

When And How To Use It

This is a *guide*book. Use it as a reference, particularly when you feel your leadership skills are being tested by a challenging situation. Reread it. This book should never get old for you. Like any book you reread, the contents may affect you in different ways the second and third time around. New lessons will emerge, minor points will take on greater importance, and its overall value will change depending on what is happening in your life and your career.

You will learn as you read and reread this guidebook, to expand the impact of your own leadership. The techniques presented will teach you how to stand before and behind your employees.

Your specific roles and responsibilities as a leader are constantly changing. The leadership model presented in this guidebook allows for this kind of change. Additionally, there is an entire chapter *(Chapter 9, The Evolving Leadership Role)* devoted to explaining appropriate roles for varied situations.

This guidebook may challenge the models you take for granted, as well as some of the ideas you've come to rely on. Read it with an open mind.

Note: We recommend you take a few moments to complete the section in the Appendix entitled "Assessing Selected Leadership Competencies." This will give you additional insight and focal points to keep in mind as you read this guidebook.

Expanding Your Impact

Much has been written over the centuries about the fundamental qualities of leaders. Personal traits and characteristics of certain individuals have been chronicled, observed, measured, and imitated. Their actions, decisions, and practices have also been scrutinized, all in the attempt to establish leadership models.

This guidebook doesn't try to recreate this work; instead, it improves the existing models by focusing on the fundamentals of leadership impact, and by incorporating the latest techniques.

There are two fundamental ways to expand your impact as a leader:

- Manage the ends and the means *(balance your goals with your methods for achieving them)*
- Build a learning team

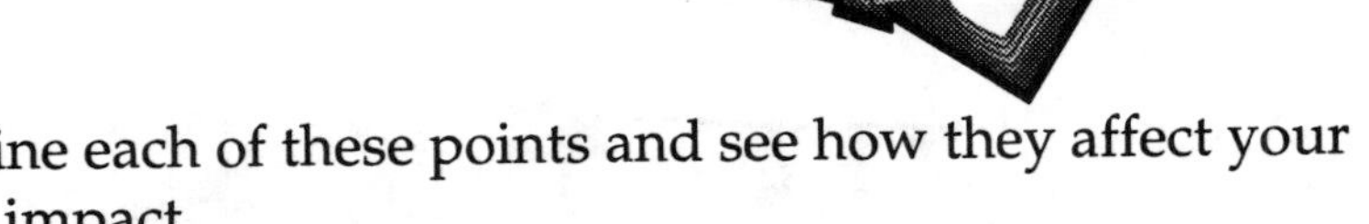

Let's examine each of these points and see how they affect your leadership impact.

Manage The Ends And The Means

A good leader understands that your goals and the ways in which you achieve them are equally important. Focusing on one to the exclusion of the other hinders team success. The two are interdependent and they need to be treated as such.

One example shows just how successful an organization can be when it balances goals and methods.

A recent study showed that . . .

when organizations focus on improving employee and customer satisfaction, their return on investments and market shares increase. The leaders of a company used this study to implement changes in their organization. The leaders focused on satisfying employees and customers *(the means),* and on increasing sales *(the ends).*

As a result of their efforts, employee morale soared to new highs, new ideas were implemented to streamline workflow *(which reduced costs and improved profits)* and stock dividends for shareholders doubled. The leaders of this company had a successful impact because they balanced their goals with their means for attaining them. . . .

Another example shows how a company made headlines by focusing on results only.

The leader of a company was . . .

concerned about improving her company's financial performance. Since this goal was paramount to her, she was willing to do anything necessary to achieve it. This included cutting company payroll and implementing strict procedures for employee breaks. However, the leader never considered how the employees would react to these changes. Well, the employees threatened to strike, and after long negotiations, they followed through with their threat by calling an 11-day strike.

The company lost approximately $50 million as a result of the strike; it shut down the company, disrupted customer service, and caused employee morale to plummet. Many customers were sympathetic to the employees and were angered by the shutdown. Many decided not to patronize the company again.

What was this leader thinking? She was focused on the end result only, with little concern shown for the means to attain that end. . . .

Focusing on the end result, such as financial performance, is only one part of leadership. Your goals and your methods in achieving them are *equally* important. However, even if there is an equal emphasis on both, you can't create success alone. Leaders need to work in conjunction with *"learning teams"*—teams that can make decisions, solve problems, and manage themselves.

Build A Learning Team

The second key to expanding leadership impact is to build a learning team. A learning team thinks for itself and doesn't depend on its leader for every decision. The team is open to new ideas, adaptable, forward-looking, and seeks ideas and opportunities to improve and innovate. A leader should form a learning team for many reasons including, but not limited to, the following:

Competitive advantage

Learning provides the best way to gain a competitive advantage. A team's ability to learn rapidly, accurately, and completely allows it to develop new skills faster than its competitors.

Adaptability

Learning improves adaptability. Teams that are adaptable develop the kind of character necessary to deal with change.

Competence and confidence

Learning builds team competence and confidence. Confidence is necessary for risk taking, and competence is required to do a job correctly the first time.

A consumer products division . . .

was able to reduce their new product approval time from 18 weeks to 24 hours. How did they do this? By changing the structure of their division from a traditional hierarchy into a dynamic learning team. Their leader was then able to facilitate a learning process where the team analyzed their own shortcomings, came up with possible solutions, tried them out, and then implemented the ones that worked best. Instead of the typical scenario where the leader makes all of the decisions, the team learned to solve their own problems. The skills and lessons they learned in this experience stayed with the team, enabling them to improve their performance in other situations they faced.

Successful leaders balance goals *(ends)* with the methods for achieving them *(means)*, and they develop their team's ability to learn on their own; these are the two fundamentals of expanding leadership impact. But they aren't skills that are acquired just by wishing. The following model provides you with guidelines of leadership impact that you can follow.

A Model For Success

The leadership model covers the essential components of successful leadership. It is not meant to be a rigid prescription. Rather, think of it as a framework on which to base your leadership decisions. For example, you may find that one of the components is more critical for your current situation than the others. If that is the case, draw from the model what you need, as you need it.

However, understanding the whole model is essential to developing a learning team, and for balancing your goals and methods for achieving them.

LEADERSHIP IMPACT MODEL

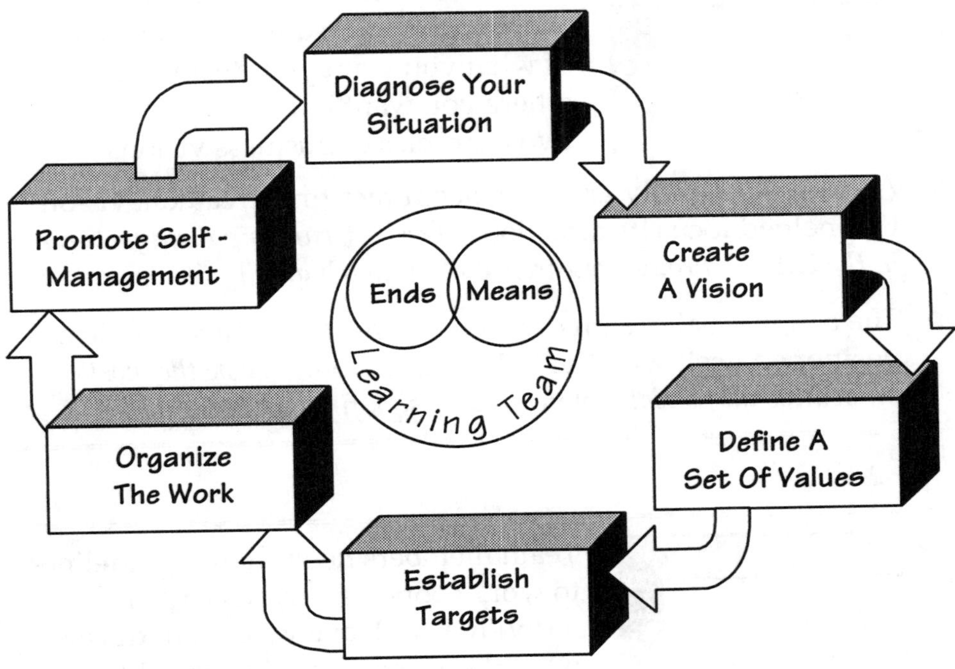

Let's take a brief look at each component:

Diagnose Your Situation

Leaders need an honest and accurate understanding of the condition of their teams to lead effectively. Use a survey or other methods to gather information that helps you understand your team's strengths and weaknesses. Following are two examples of leaders learning about the conditions of their teams.

- A restaurant manager conducted brief meetings with her waiters and waitresses on each shift to discuss the overall effectiveness of their teams.
- A manufacturing director, having gathered feedback via an anonymous survey on how his management team was doing, identified that the team needed clearer, more measurable targets for their work.

Create A Vision

People need direction to be motivated. Work with your team to create a picture of what you want your team to do and where you want it to go. Following are two examples of business visions.

- A small but rapidly growing electronics firm created a vision that helped focus its direction: *"The best-run chip manufacturer in the U.S.A. through research and top-notch quality."*
- The commercial design division of a major architecture firm positioned itself with the following vision: *"To be the most innovative industrial architectural design firm in the world."*

Define A Set Of Values

Team members need shared guidelines to work cooperatively instead of individually. Have your team develop what these *"ground rules"* should be. Here are examples of what two teams did:

- An accounting firm's employees sought to establish a collective work ethic. They decided that integrity, trust and sincerity were their core values for dealing with each other and their customers.
- A metropolitan utility determined that four critical values would guide their operations. They were: a *"can-do,"* problem solving attitude, all customers are equal, no *"short-cuts,"* and always apply the long-term solution.

People respond to specific challenges and goals. Clearly convey the quality of the product or service you want your team to produce, and ways to quantify your team's progress.

- An athletic equipment manufacturer determined that two key measurable quality targets were critical to increasing market share. They were: all product characteristics must be clearly visible to the customer *(color, shape, texture, etc.)* while meeting specifications within 5percent; and returns for performance defects or breakage must not exceed one per thousand.
- A leading advertising agency set the following targets for assessing customer needs: onsite visits and interviews with active clients every month; and structured phone interviews with every inactive client (*with whom the organization has not worked with during the year*) every three months.

Organize The Work

People want to have some control over how and in what order they do their work. Teach your team the essential skills for organizing the workflow so they can achieve their targets. Here's what two teams did:

- A garden tools manufacturer, analyzed its workflow for manufacturing wooden handles. The organization learned that quality control procedures for receiving raw incoming wood stock were vaguely written and largely ignored. This resulted in a large number of rejects after tooling due to wood defects. So, they enhanced their wood stock procedures and achieved an 80 percent defect reduction.
- A chemical laboratory discovered that cross-training manufacturing workers to assist in all areas reduced overall downtime by 25 percent, thus shortening their order-to-ship time window.

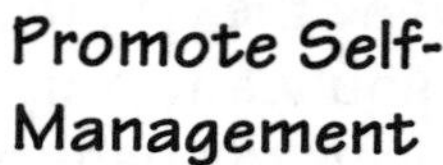

People like to make their own decisions and accept responsibility for them. If you have a vision, set of values, clear targets, and an organized workflow, then your team will have the confidence to make its own decisions. Thus, your team will begin managing itself, and consequently, fulfilling your goals. Take a look at the following examples.

- A large real estate agency, with a reputation for punishing staff who try innovative home financing approaches that sometimes fail, decided to change its ways. The organization began to: reward those with successful new ideas, and objectively analyze innovative failures rather than punish employees. They achieved a 30 percent increase in business within one year.

- A luggage manufacturer eliminated its quality control department by delegating all quality control responsibility to the various product work teams, thus reducing costs and product defects. The work teams were reluctant at first, but soon embraced the opportunities to *"call the shots"* in managing for quality results.

Now that you have been introduced to the elements of the leadership model, each one will be fully discussed in the following chapters.

Chapter Two Worksheet: Understanding Your Leadership Impact

1. What situations have you observed or been involved in where the leader's focus on results and the methods used to achieve them were unbalanced?

2. What would you have done differently in those situations?

3. What situations have you observed or been involved in where the leader created a learning team?

4. What were some of the results?

5. Which components of the leadership model will immediately expand your leadership impact? Why?

6. What are the potential hurdles for expanding your leadership impact?

Diagnose Your Situation

Leaders need an honest and accurate understanding of their current situation to lead effectively. Consider:

- The extent of your leadership impact
- The effectiveness with which you are managing both ends and the means to achieve those ends
- How much your team is learning

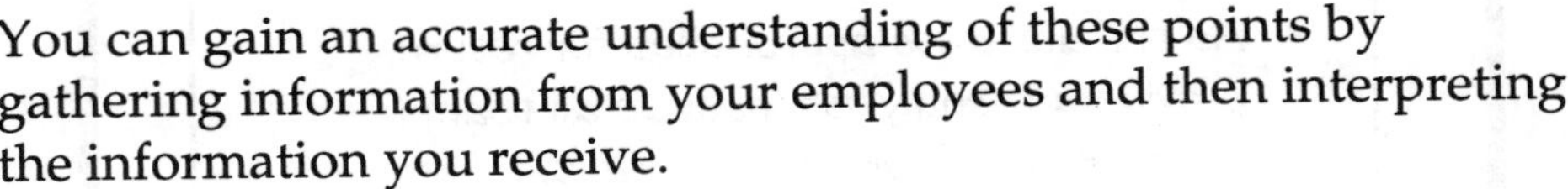

You can gain an accurate understanding of these points by gathering information from your employees and then interpreting the information you receive.

Gather Information From Your Employees

The people you are leading are the best source of information about your team's current situation and your impact as their leader. One way to gather information from them is to use an informal survey. These surveys are relatively easy to create, distribute, and collect.

The following points can help you to develop, implement, and collect an informal survey.

- Determine who will fill out the survey.
- Draft the survey, including an explanation of why you are requesting it. *(See the sample survey for items you may want to include.)*
- If many team members are involved, have a few members complete the survey in a *"pilot"* test and ask them how you could improve it.
- Revise and distribute the survey, providing ample time for completion and return.
- As the due date approaches for return, provide a friendly reminder to all team members *(everyone's busy, right?)*.
- Phone calls or visits may be required to *"chase down"* all of the surveys.

Following is an example of such a survey.

Team Situation Survey

Respond to the following statements by circling the appropriate number on a scale of 1 to 5. Your honest responses are important to your team's performance.

1	3	5
Strongly disagree	Neither agree nor disagree	Strongly agree

1. I have a clear vision of what our team is working towards.	**1 2 3 4 5**
2. This vision provides a sense of purpose.	**1 2 3 4 5**
3. The vision is *"motivating."*	**1 2 3 4 5**
4. I think the vision is the *"right"* vision.	**1 2 3 4 5**
Subtotal	
5. I have a clear understanding of our team's *"ground rules."*	**1 2 3 4 5**
6. These rules are important.	**1 2 3 4 5**
7. I follow these rules.	**1 2 3 4 5**
8. The rules are appropriate for every member of our team.	**1 2 3 4 5**
Subtotal	
9. The existing team is effective.	**1 2 3 4 5**
10. Our team's organization is consistent with the vision.	**1 2 3 4 5**
11. Our team's organization facilitates communication.	**1 2 3 4 5**
12. Employees can change the workflow as needed.	**1 2 3 4 5**
Subtotal	
13. Our team has clearly defined targets.	**1 2 3 4 5**
14. The targets are reasonable.	**1 2 3 4 5**
15. The targets are consistent with the vision.	**1 2 3 4 5**
16. Mistakes are treated as learning opportunities.	**1 2 3 4 5**
Subtotal	
17. Leader allows employees to be self-managing.	**1 2 3 4 5**
18. Employees are encouraged to solve problems.	**1 2 3 4 5**
19. Leader provides constructive feedback.	**1 2 3 4 5**
20. Leader rewards performance.	**1 2 3 4 5**
Total	

Jane, a leader of a product development team, . . .
asked her employees to complete the Team Situation Survey. *"No one has to put their name on the survey,"* she said, *"just be certain to respond. If you like, you can turn them in to a designated person on the team."* The team elected John to receive, score, and deliver the surveys to Jane. John received fourteen of the fifteen surveys by the end of the week. Jane's next step was to interpret the information on the surveys. . . .

Interpret The Information

One way to interpret the information you receive is to compare each survey to the scorecard. For each survey you receive, total all of the points. Calculate the average for the completed questionnaire. Locate this average within the corresponding range on the scorecard; this will help you gauge your overall effectiveness.

Scorecard

90 to 100: You are effectively managing both means and ends and your team is functioning as a learning team. You and your team can continue to excel by committing to memory your "practices," and looking for new ideas to avoid becoming complacent.

75 to 89: Your ability to manage the means and the ends is definitely above average. Assess the subtotal scores to identify any area of weakness for you. This may be an area where you will have to learn new techniques to enhance your impact and build a learning team.

60 to 74: You could be having a much greater leadership impact. Your vision and values may not be as clear as you believe them to be. Are you making many decisions yourself instead of enabling your team to think on their own? Is it possible that your targets and organization of the work are hindering team effectiveness and increasing frustration? Many leaders begin with scores in this category and find that by making immediate, small changes in several areas they can really improve their scores.

Less than 60: You are not having a successful impact as a leader; take this information to heart! At this level, it's important to look at each question on the survey. Take full advantage of the leadership model. Start by working with your employees to clarify the vision and establish a realistic set of values. It's likely that problems with the vision and values may be contributing to the lower scores you see in organization, targets, and self-management (Questions 9 to 20).

The next step in interpreting the survey is to identify low scoring areas that correspond to the elements in the leadership model: the vision, values, targets, work, and self-management practices. Look for scores that are below average in these areas. By concentrating on the lowest scoring areas, you can dramatically improve your overall leadership impact.

Jane prides herself on . . .

maintaining open and direct communication with her team members, but she was still surprised at the results of the survey. The average total score was 73, but she noticed consistently low scores on certain questions. The average score on Questions 17 to 20 was a "2." Jane thought she always encouraged her employees to be self-managing and to solve their own problems, so she was shocked by these results. She was most distressed by the scores on constructive feedback and rewards *(Questions 19 and 20).* She believed she was a good coach, but she scored a "1" on both of these questions. Was she mistaken about her own leadership impact? She decided to find out more by asking for direct feedback from the group.

Her team members responded by telling her that, overall, she was a good person to work for; they all agreed that she did a great job of creating a vision, setting targets, and organizing the workflow. However, they felt that she did not truly abide by the team's established guidelines, such as *"taking initiative," "developing personal skills,"* or *"trying innovative ideas."* They told her that despite her best intentions, she was very controlling; she didn't allow them to take chances or make decisions. Some of the team members stated that they were becoming bored. The present atmosphere wasn't challenging and didn't offer learning opportunities. Because of their responses, Jane decided to change. She asked herself, *"What should I be doing differently to become a more effective leader?"*

Diagnosing your own situation can be difficult. Your emotions and your employees' emotions are both involved, and you might receive information critical of your current leadership approach. However, don't let this possibility prevent you from conducting the survey.

There are many ways to gather information from team members, depending on the size of the team, your relationship with team members, the importance of confidentiality, and so forth. You may want to try:

- One-on-one interviews (often successful with employees whose cultures do not encourage openness in groups)
- Team meetings
- Impartial meetings, facilitated by someone outside of the team in your absence
- Offsite meetings, which may reduce distractions and enhance open communication
- Phone surveys

Regardless of how you gather the information, it is imperative to ask these questions if you are to provide competent, quality leadership. Obtaining feedback on the current situation and your leadership role is a crucial first step.

CHAPTER THREE WORKSHEET: FINDING OUT WHERE YOU STAND

1. How will you gather information about your present leadership impact?

2. If you are going to use a survey, what questions do you need to ask? *(**Note:** you can photocopy and use the sample survey in the Appendix, if appropriate, or adapt it to your specific situation.)*

3. Who will administer the survey? Who will process it? How will anonymity be handled?

4. How will the information be summarized and presented to you?

5. How will you interpret the information?

6. Who will you share this interpretation with? How? When? Where?

CREATE A VISION

People need meaning to be motivated and inspired. One of the greatest leadership challenges is to provide a purpose for the work that your employees do. People like to know that they are part of something bigger than themselves and that they have a hand in shaping it.

A vision is always necessary, even when it may not seem so. For example, when two different organizations are in a highly competitive situation, people in each organization naturally seem to rally together to win. Similarly, in a start-up situation, there is often an initial sense of shared enthusiasm and focus. Are these organizations winning without visions? No. Their vision for the moment is a combination of winning and surviving. Yet it's likely that the competitor with the clearest vision will win. And it's likely that a small organization will not grow much larger without a vision.

What Is A Vision?

A vision describes how the future is supposed to look. A vision provides people with a framework to make and understand:

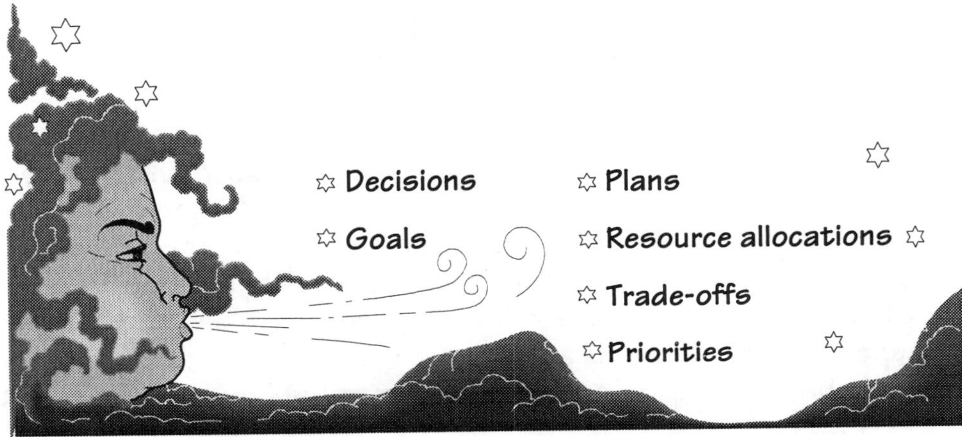

But visions are useful only if your team members understand their roles in them. You are probably accustomed to seeing vision statements phrased in the following forms:

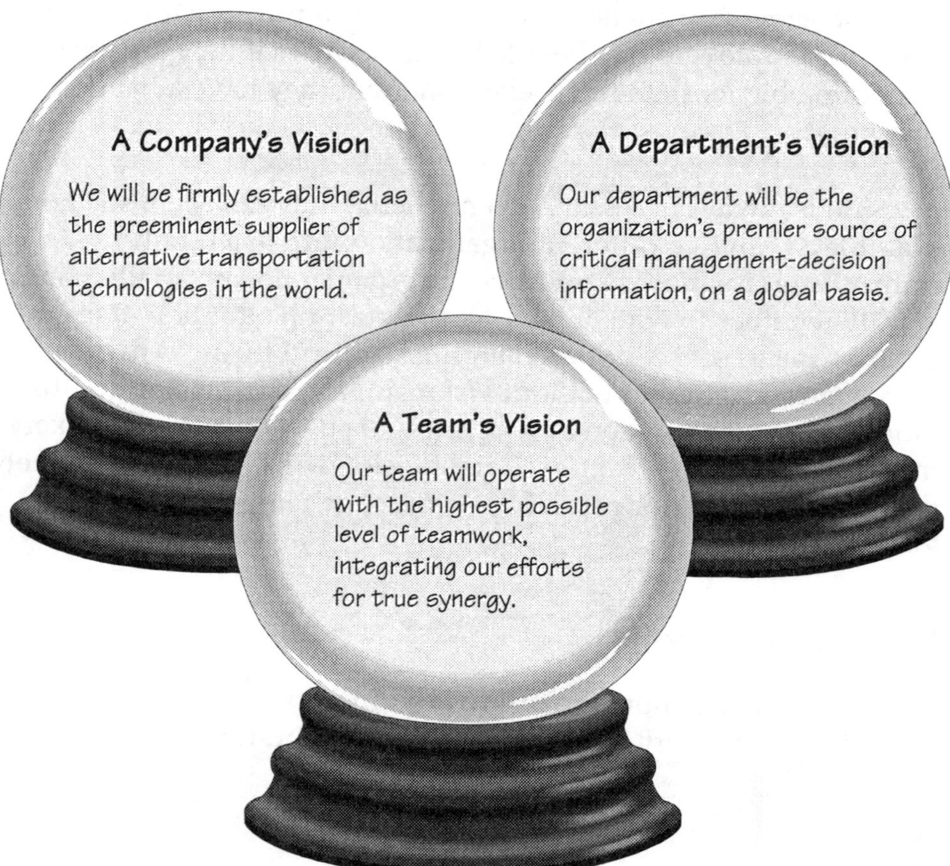

A Company's Vision
We will be firmly established as the preeminent supplier of alternative transportation technologies in the world.
A Department's Vision
Our department will be the organization's premier source of critical management-decision information, on a global basis.
A Team's Vision
Our team will operate with the highest possible level of teamwork, integrating our efforts for true synergy.

Do these visions provide a meaning and a purpose for employees? Do these visions define the employees' roles in fulfilling them? The answer to these questions is *"No."* These visions might have good intentions, but they are not as effective as they should be. We will show you how to form potent, strongly-worded vision statements; statements that communicate a story to unfold in the future and explain how your team members will contribute to this future.

Creating such visions is a two-part process:

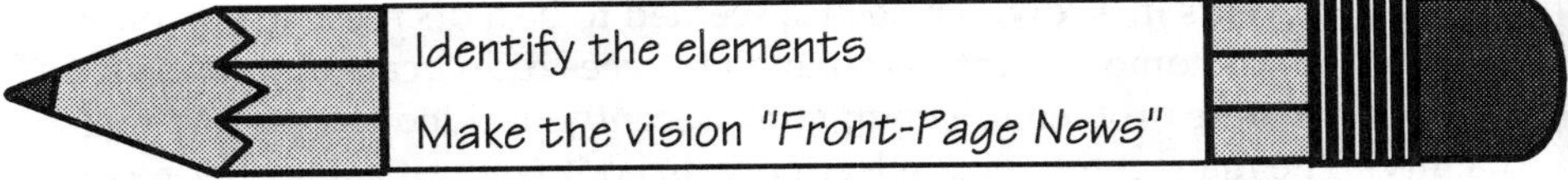

Identify The Elements

The first step in creating your vision is to determine what the individual elements of the vision should be. Answer the following questions; your answers will be the critical elements to include in your vision.

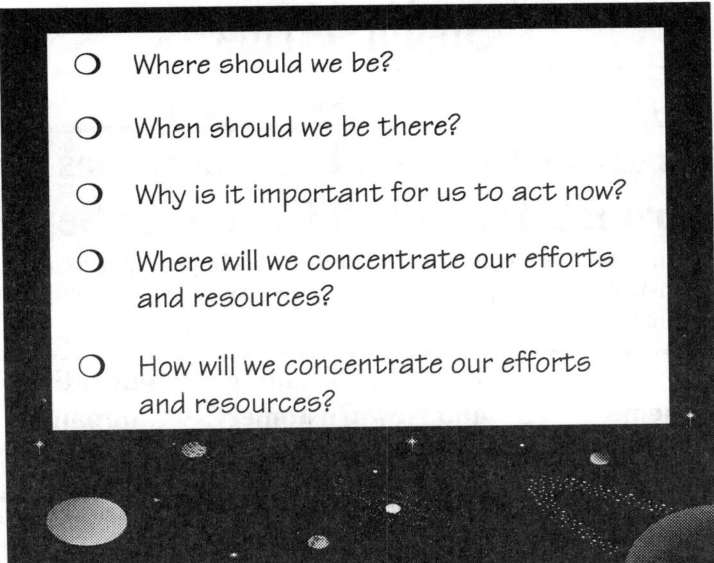

Where should we be?
When should we be there?
Why is it important for us to act now?
Where will we concentrate our efforts and resources?
How will we concentrate our efforts and resources?

Make The Vision "Front-Page News"

The second step in creating your vision is to combine the individual elements into a unified whole. Write your vision down on paper, covering all of the critical points you answered in the first step. It's important to do this since information is best conveyed visually. The more visual your communication, the higher the retention value—this is what we call *"Making Front-Page News."*

The leader of a ski resort management team . . .

had a problem: the resort's financial status was tenuous. Revenue had been flat for two years in a row. The cause seemed to be a decrease in customer satisfaction; customers perceived that employees didn't care about service. To compound these problems, a competitor recently decided to upgrade their facility. The management team leader realized it was critical for her resort's survival to improve customer service. She also realized that she needed to create a clear and specific vision of a successful future—a vision all employees could understand and identify with.

Thus, she met with her entire management team and facilitated the two-part process. First they identified the elements of the vision. Then, they wrote a story that would *"Make Front-Page News."* The following is their team's vision.

Vision News

CIRCULATION:
1,138,353 DAILY 1,521,197 SUNDAY **THURSDAY, FEBRUARY 10, 19XX**

Best Resort In The U.S. Increases Sales Through Improved Customer Service

After two years of flat revenues, the resort reported a 20 percent increase in revenue. Customer satisfaction has improved by more than 30 percent. Much of the credit goes to the ski school that led the change in customer service policies.

Facility Improvement

By MICHAEL JONES
STAFF WRITER

Customers and employees frequently complained about the *"user unfriendliness"* of the resort facilities. Employees got together and solved the problem. A computer system was installed to make it easier for customers to use the resort facilities and amenities. Based on the positive results, the resort is considering a $25 million expenditure to upgrade the facilities next year.

Employee Training and New Customer Service Program

By JANE SMITH
STAFF WRITER

In the past, high employee turnover and poor customer service tarnished the resort's reputation. After a two-year effort to train employees and managers in customer service, a management reorganization, and a change in worker compensation policies, employee turnover has decreased and customer satisfaction has increased. This is good news for managers, whose new compensation program rewards them for customer satisfaction, employee retention, and sales.

Innovative Campaigns

By SUZANNE BOOTH
STAFF WRITER

Competition was hurting the resort. A team of employees worked on implementing several programs to beat the competition. Especially effective were commercials that emphasized the resort's amenities and new customer service policies, and the development of a frequent visitor program.

In this example, the management team leader packaged the vision in a poster-size newspaper format. She posted it on every wall in employee areas. And she used it as a working vision; a document that is discussed at meetings and used for both short and long-term planning.

This kind of vision provided a clear picture for resort employees.

The visioning process addressed these critical elements:

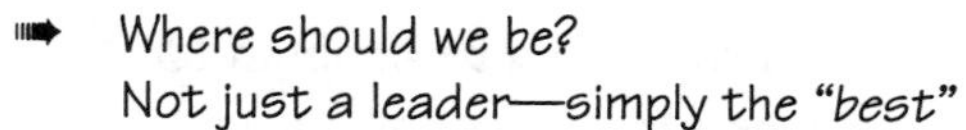

- Where should we be?
  Not just a leader—simply the *"best"*

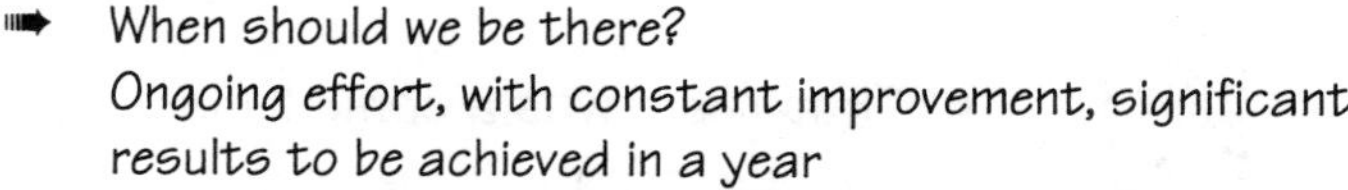

- When should we be there?
  Ongoing effort, with constant improvement, significant results to be achieved in a year
- Why is it important for us to act now?
  Flat revenue, decreased customer satisfaction, competitor upgrades
- Where will we concentrate our efforts and resources?
  Improved customer service

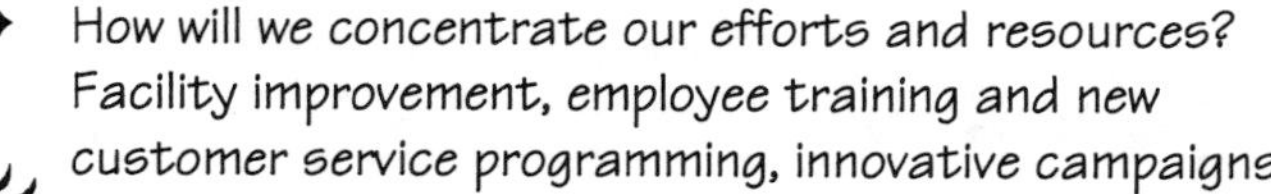

- How will we concentrate our efforts and resources?
  Facility improvement, employee training and new customer service programming, innovative campaigns

Not only did it convey a purpose, provide meaning, and communicate employee roles, everyone understood:

- Specific goals of the vision
- How they could make more money
- What needed to happen to make their jobs more secure
- That they would be trained to take on new responsibilities
- That there was a commitment to improve the facilities

Chapter Four Worksheet: Creating Your Vision

1. Answer the following questions. *(Your answers will form the individual elements of your vision.)*

a) Where should we be?

b) When should we be there?

c) Why is it important for us to act now?

d) Where will we concentrate our efforts and resources?

e) How will we concentrate our efforts and resources?

2. Draft your vision.

3. How will you make your vision *"Front-Page News"?*

4. Revise your vision to incorporate input from other critical contributors.

DEFINE A SET OF VALUES

Team members need shared guidelines to work cooperatively instead of individually. Your responsibility as the leader is to help your team decide what these guidelines (*ground rules)* should be.

Another way to look at guidelines is think of them as values that:

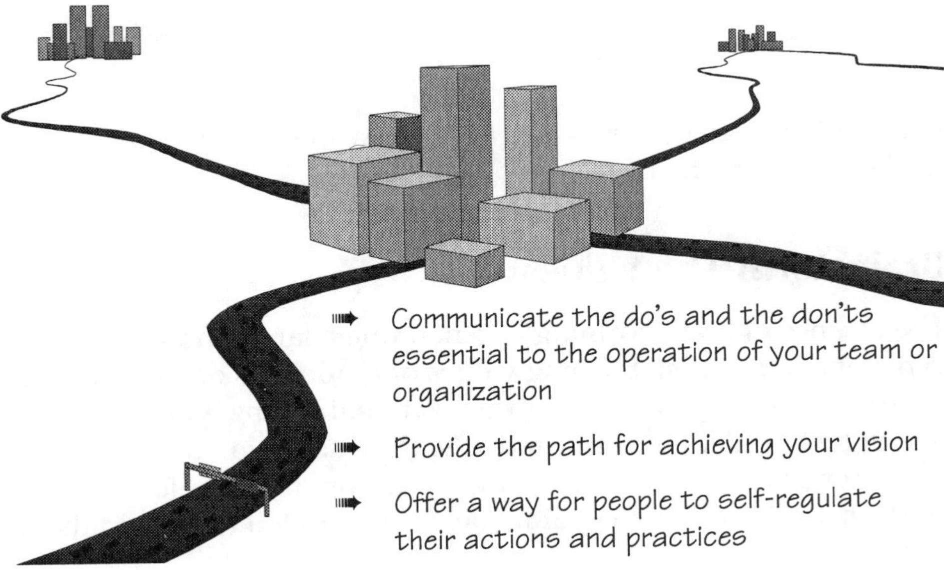

- Communicate the do's and the don'ts essential to the operation of your team or organization
- Provide the path for achieving your vision
- Offer a way for people to self-regulate their actions and practices

How important is it to have defined values? Some organizations have discovered the importance of defined values the hard way. Visions accomplished at the expense of values can have a disastrous outcome.

In one case, . . .

an auto repair company's vision made it clear that connecting compensation to store performance would produce more profit, sales, and money for store managers. Within a year of taking steps to implement the vision, the company was indicted on charges of overbilling and cheating customers. A value system that made it clear these kinds of behaviors were unacceptable might have prevented this company's reputation from being ruined. . . .

Use the following steps to develop a set of values for your team.

- Brainstorm the values
- Decide on the *"right"* values for your team
- Define the values
- Promote the values

Let's look at each of these steps to see how they affect your leadership impact.

Brainstorm The Values

The essence of brainstorming is generating a large number of ideas. When it comes to establishing values or guidelines on how people are expected to operate in an organizational setting, you can be sure everyone has ideas to contribute. As the leader, you drive the brainstorming process—receiving input from the people who will be deeply affected by the guidelines and expected to uphold them.

Here are a few questions that are useful in starting your brainstorming session:

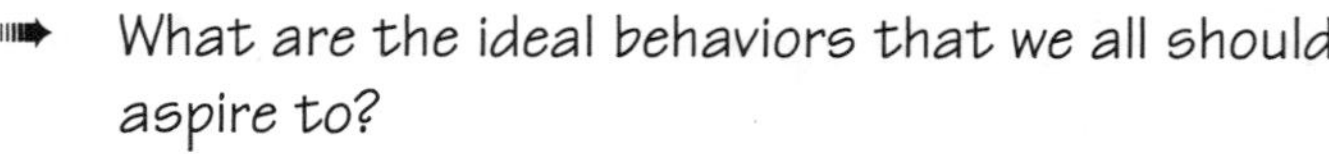

What are the ideal behaviors that we all should aspire to?

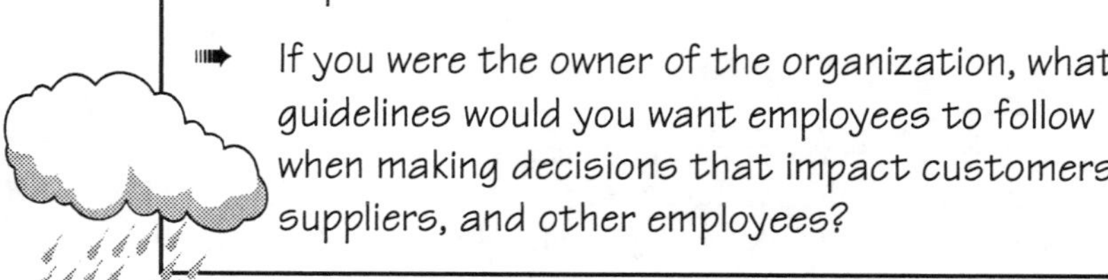

If you were the owner of the organization, what guidelines would you want employees to follow when making decisions that impact customers, suppliers, and other employees?

Glen, the leader . . .

of a highly successful retail organization, conducted several brainstorming sessions with groups of employees to generate a list of ideas for the organization's values. After brainstorming with dozens of people, their list contained the following values:

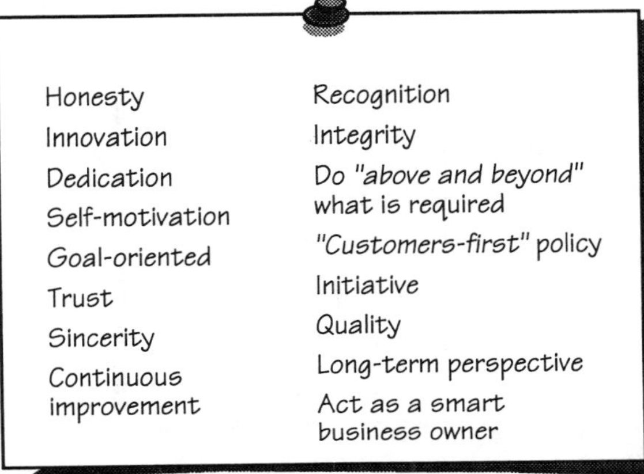

Honesty
Innovation
Dedication
Self-motivation
Goal-oriented
Trust
Sincerity
Continuous improvement
Recognition
Integrity
Do *"above and beyond"* what is required
"Customers-first" policy
Initiative
Quality
Long-term perspective
Act as a smart business owner

Decide On The "Right" Values For Your Team

After brainstorming for ideas, the next step is for your team to decide which values are appropriate. The *"right"* values should:

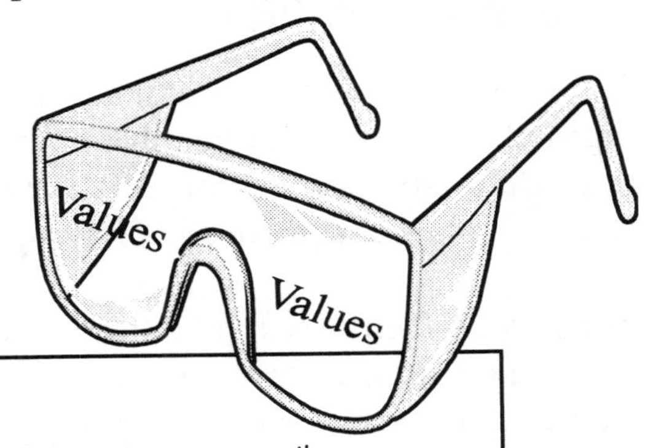

- Directly support the vision; not necessarily reflect the *"as is"*
- Complement existing organization's values
- Be regarded as important by a majority of the team members

Glen decided . . .

to organize two focus groups, open to anyone interested in deciding which values the organization was going to adopt. He thought the discussions would be wide-ranging, and that it might take some pushing on his part to come to an agreement. But, to his surprise, the groups arrived at a consensus fairly quickly, and produced a list of six values:

Innovation
Teamwork
Quality
Integrity
Continuous improvement
Initiative

One point that came up repeatedly in the discussions was the need to have clear definitions for each value. Otherwise, people would read their own meanings into the words. Glen realized this next step was an important one. . . .

Define The Values

For a set of values to have an impact, they need to be clearly defined. There should be minimal room for interpretation, because that could lead to misinterpretation or conflicting interpretations, which defeats the purpose of having guidelines.

The most effective way to define your team's values is to write out a sentence or two supporting each value, followed by specific examples of how each value is important in everyday situations. The specific examples can be written in terms of suggested *"do's"* and *"don'ts."*

INNOVATION:

We encourage and reward creativity. As a leader in change, we are always open to new ideas to improve performance.

ON-THE-JOB BEHAVIORS:

- Make suggestions
- Don't give up when people don't listen at first
- If your ideas are not well received, improve them and present them again

ON-THE-JOB BEHAVIORS (continued):

- Don't get hung up on the *"not invented here"* syndrome
- Take appropriate risks by working with people to change the system
- Don't settle for *"good enough"*
- Don't let mistakes stop the process

TEAMWORK:

We encourage idea-sharing, common goals and departmental unity. We promote these things by involving employees in the decision-making and problem-solving processes.

ON-THE-JOB BEHAVIORS:

- Talk in terms of specific product and service needs and wants
- Develop/share goals, defining specific outputs

ON-THE-JOB BEHAVIORS (continued):

- Don't draft goals without input
- Link individual goals with interdepartmental goals
- Don't be a maverick without a good reason
- Share responsibilities

QUALITY:

We provide value to our customers by performing consistently and reliably. We maintain a competitive advantage by *"designing-in"* quality, setting high standards, and producing defect-free work.

ON-THE-JOB BEHAVIORS:

- Do it right the first time by checking your own work
- Never pass on a product with a defect or error
- Ask your customer what they want

ON-THE-JOB BEHAVIORS (continued):

- Tell your suppliers what you need
- Don't assume that others understand your needs
- Address quality problems immediately
- Solicit feedback from your customers
- Meet with customers and suppliers
- Treat customers as individuals

INTEGRITY:

We conduct ourselves at all times with honesty, trustworthiness, and open and direct communication.

ON-THE-JOB BEHAVIORS:

- *"Practice what you preach"*
- Don't make unreasonable promises
- Be honest about problems
- Don't circulate rumors
- Praise as much as you criticize

CONTINUOUS IMPROVEMENT:

We set high expectations for ourselves and identify ways to go the *"extra mile"* for our customers. We evaluate our work processes daily to identify areas that need improvement.

ON-THE-JOB BEHAVIORS:

- We look for opportunities for improvement, however small
- We recognize that everything can be improved upon

ON-THE-JOB BEHAVIORS (continued):

- Our internal improvements eventually lead to improvements for our customers
- Continuous improvement means there will be moving targets

INITIATIVE:

We start things rather than wait for someone else to do it for us. We try to anticipate problems before they occur.

ON-THE-JOB BEHAVIORS:

- When you come up with an idea, do something with it
- Initiative involves risk, don't stifle an initiative because of risk
- Quantify it first, then decide

ON-THE-JOB BEHAVIORS (continued):

- Share your new ways of doing things with others
- Be open to other people's suggestions

Promote The Values

The most important part of defining your set of values is *promotion*. Your values are useless if they are not seen. As a leader, what you do to promote and instill the values will determine whether people really take them to heart or just pay them lip service.

Ways to promote your values include:

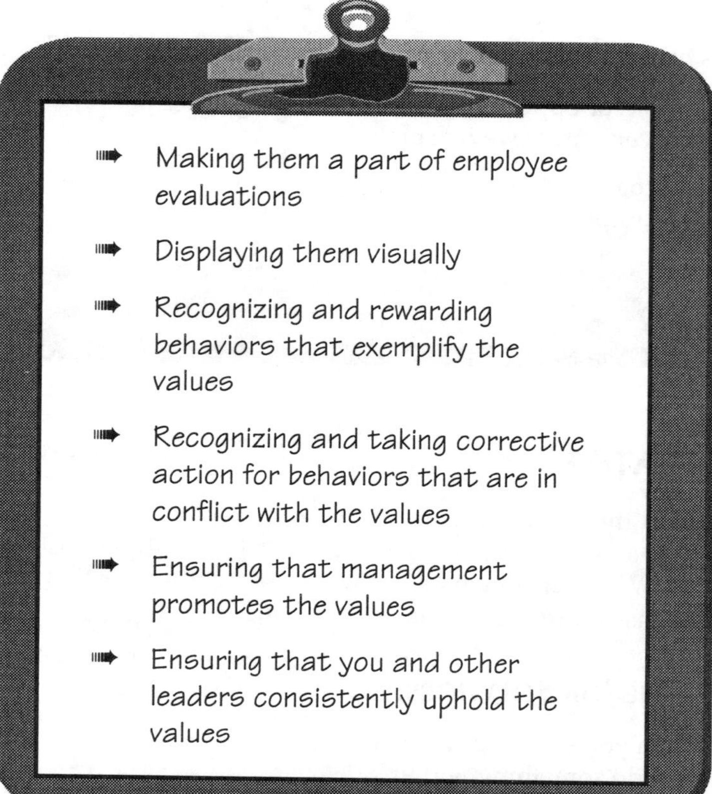

Making them a part of employee evaluations
Displaying them visually
Recognizing and rewarding behaviors that exemplify the values
Recognizing and taking corrective action for behaviors that are in conflict with the values
Ensuring that management promotes the values
Ensuring that you and other leaders consistently uphold the values

Glen met with his top managers . . .

to confirm that they understood the importance of each value. He then instructed the managers to discuss the importance and meaning of their values in one-on-one meetings with each employee. The initial reaction from the senior managers was concern over the amount of time these meetings would require.

His response was, *"If we expect the people who work for this company to take these values to heart and uphold them on a daily basis, they need to see that we take them very seriously too. We need to demonstrate how important this is to the company, and I'm convinced this is the way to do it."* After more discussion, the group agreed to hold their one-on-one meetings over the next two weeks.

Chapter Five Worksheet
Establishing Your Team's Values

1. Who will be involved in brainstorming values for your team or organization?

___

___

___

2. What examples or questions will you use to start the brainstorming?

___

___

___

3. Brainstorm a list of at least 20 possible values.

___

___

___

___

___

___

___

4. Which of your brainstormed values are the *"right"* ones for you? *(Hint: narrow your list down to about five or six.)*

5. Define each value and provide examples showing how each value is important in everyday situations.

6. As the leader, how will you ensure that the values are promoted?

ESTABLISH TARGETS

Employees respond to the challenges of reaching targets. People are motivated by challenges when they believe they have a chance to succeed; they remain motivated when they can see the results of their efforts. Leaders can create and maintain motivation by establishing targets and reviewing progress frequently.

Remember the two fundamentals of leadership impact discussed earlier: manage the ends and the means, and build a learning team? The way a leader establishes and tracks progress against targets has a direct link to these two points.

- Leaders establish targets as a common reference point to focus on the ends.

- When targets are clear, specific, and understood by all, the means to achieve them also become clearer. Thus, clear targets lead to more easily defined and understood methods and processes.

- Individuals with clear targets are much more apt to become a learning team than people facing ambiguous targets *(goals).* With clarity comes purpose, and with purpose comes the willingness to try new approaches and acquire new skills, essentially to develop into a learning team.

Your role as a leader is to visualize and convey a picture of your team's goals. Link your targets to your vision, to the work, and by using variances from targets, to identify problem-solving opportunities.

The following three steps are presented in this chapter as a means for you to lead your team in establishing targets.

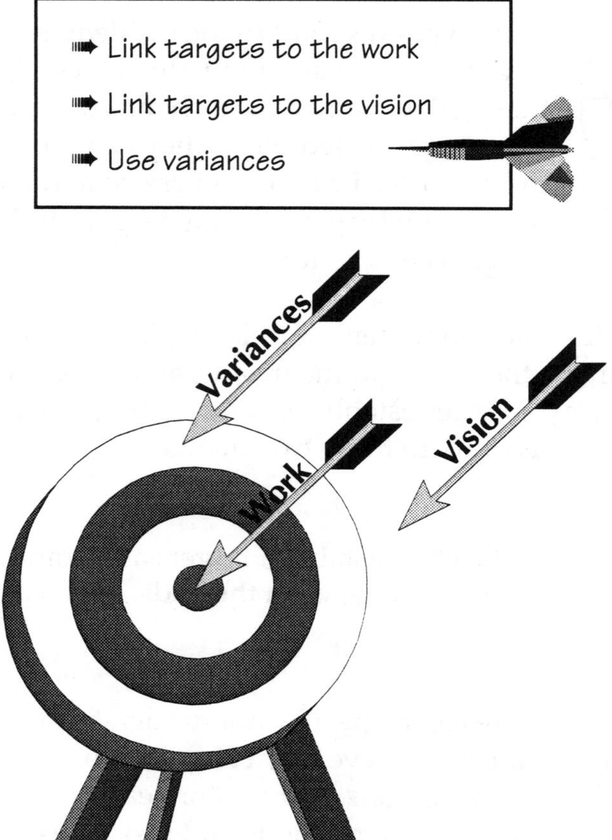

Link Targets To The Work

Teams exist to provide a product or service. Team targets should be directly linked to the quality of the product or service.

For example, suppose a product development team designs products that other divisions in the same organization must make, sell, deliver, and service. The quality of the product they produce might be measured in the time it took to develop the product from start to finish *(the faster the better)*, the cost required to develop it *(the less the better)*, and the sales it generates *(the more the better)*.

Julia, the product development team leader, set targets for:

- **Time-to-market:** measured by how long it takes them to translate an idea into a product and a marketing plan
- **Development cost:** measured in terms of a ratio of gross profit to overhead expense
- **Financial returns:** measured by the ratio of new sales to development cost
- **Customer satisfaction:** measured by customer response surveys

To help you determine appropriate targets for your team, ask yourself the following questions:

The answers to these questions and others will lead to the answer to another question, *"Which targets should be set, and why?"*

Generally, specific targets will fall into the following categories:

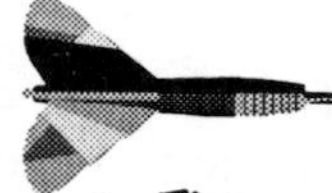

- **Time**—how long it takes to make a product or provide a service
- **Cost**—how much it takes to make the product or provide the service
- **Satisfaction**—the satisfaction customers experience with the end product or service; and the satisfaction employees experience in producing/providing it
- **Financial**—the *"bottom-line"* benefits generated by producing or providing it

Leaders recognize that almost all products or services need to have specifically defined targets. But how do you know which are the right or best targets? One way is to apply the 80/20 rule, where focusing on the right 20 percent of your targets, or problems, will most likely bring you 80 percent improvement.

You can identify these key targets or problems by determining which ones, if achieved or resolved, would make the most improvements in:

- Customer satisfaction
- Reduced costs of production or service
- Workflow efficiency
- Overall quality
- Employee satisfaction
- Net profit

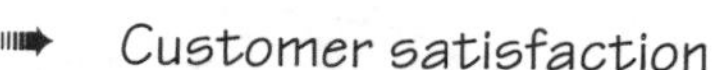

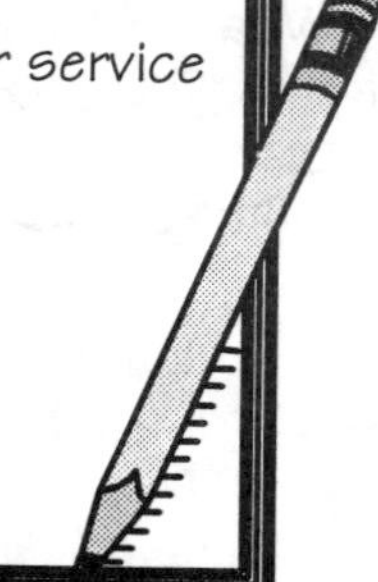

Customers and employees are the best source for helping prioritize and measure these high-return targets.

Keep in mind that the most important criteria in establishing targets is to make sure they are linked to the team's vision.

Link Targets To The Vision

Teams are held together and driven by their measurement systems. So, it is important to measure the right things. Targets that are not linked to, and consistent with, your vision create confusion for your team.

For example, one bank's vision included a dedication to, and a focus on, customer service. However, the bank measured success in terms of asset growth and net profit. Nowhere was there any measurement or target for customer satisfaction. When faced with a decision between customer service and profits, employees responded by making decisions that improved profits, sacrificing customer service. Why? Because that's what was measured and targeted. Your targets need to be linked to your vision.

To link your targets to your vision, set up a matrix comparing the specific targets with elements of the vision. *(Remember, the vision included specific, quantitative measures of success.)* For example, Julia's product development team arrived at some interesting conclusions using the following matrix diagram.

Vision and Target Matrix

	PRODUCT/SERVICE TARGETS			
ELEMENTS OF OUR VISION	TARGET # 1 **Time-to-market** *(maximum of 40 weeks for average projects, target of 15 weeks for fast-track projects)*	TARGET # 2 **Development cost** *(Set on a case-by-case basis)*	TARGET # 3 **Financial returns** *(Payback period of 18 months or less, and margins of 40%)*	TARGET # 4 **Customer satisfaction** *(80% high interest/ satisfaction level in focus groups; 85% post launch)*
Return on investment of 18%	◒	●	●	●
New products 40% of sales	●	◒	◒	●
Three new products launched	●	◒	◒	●

● = Strong impact ◒ = Medium impact ○ = Little impact

Julia and her team members . . .
compared the elements of their vision against their product/service targets and discovered that the two were indeed well linked. The solid circles indicate strong impact on, and linkage of, the specific product/services targets with elements of the vision. The half-circles indicate medium impact, and an open circle indicates little impact and linkage. This was a happy result. The team seemed to be measuring the right things.

They soon discovered, however, that they had set two of their targets too low. The time-to-market and the development cost targets were set at levels insufficient to fulfill their vision. . . .

Use Variances

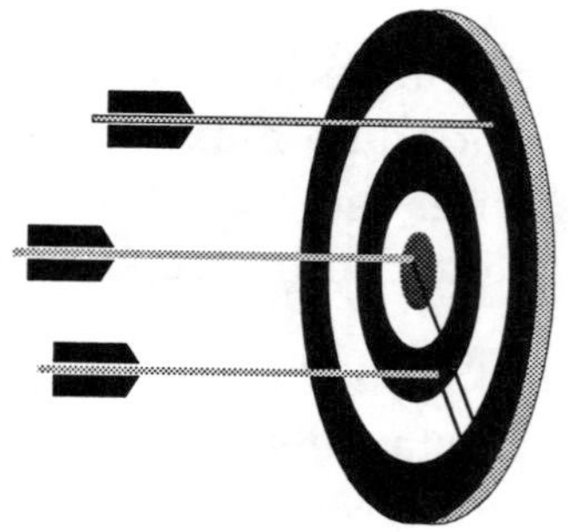

Remember, both positive and negative results can strengthen a team. Reaching target levels validates employees' work and gives them a sense of accomplishment. Effective leaders lavish praise on team members when they meet their targets. They don't take success for granted. However, the best opportunity for learning is when targets aren't achieved. Effective leaders refrain from assigning blame for target shortfalls; instead, they challenge their teams to understand the reasons behind their shortfalls and to search for solutions.

Julia got together with . . .
her team to reset their targets. The time-to-market was going to be the most challenging. They were going to have to dramatically change the way they organized their work to accomplish the time-to-market target.

Julia always kept in mind that people respond to challenges and goals, and stay motivated when they can clearly see the results of their efforts. She felt like she was doing the right things in setting the kinds of targets that would focus the actions and behaviors of her team.

Chapter Six Worksheet: Establish Your Targets

1. Use the following questions *(and others appropriate for your situation)* to focus on establishing and selecting targets.

a) Who are your customers?

b) What do you sell them?

c) What targets are important to them?

d) What's the quality of your product or service?

2. Based on your answers to the previous questions, set specific targets for the following:

a) Time

b) Cost

c) Satisfaction

d) Financial

3. Use a matrix to compare your targets with specific elements of your vision.

Note: There is also a blank matrix in the Appendix for you to photocopy and use.

	Product/Service Targets			
Elements of Our Vision	Target # 1	Target # 2	Target # 3	Target # 4

● = Strong impact ◒ = Medium impact ○ = Little impact

ORGANIZE THE WORK

People want to know what to do in their work. They also want to have some control over how they do it. Clarity and ownership promote efficiency and effectiveness of work efforts. Leaders manage the means and build a learning team by getting people actively involved in the design and organization of their work.

For example, here's a situation where a lack of employee involvement in organizing the workflow actually hindered efficiency and effectiveness.

The employees of an airline . . .
staged a work *"slowdown"* without striking or calling in sick. In staging their slowdown, the employees followed all work procedures, rules, and chains of command *"to the letter."* As a result of the slowdown, the company's operations came to a halt. The only way to correct the situation was for the company to allow employees to adopt more efficient, informal procedures. In other words, there was a serious discrepancy between the way things really got done *(the informal process)* and the way it was supposed to be done *(the formal process).* Once the employees were allowed to redesign the workflow, the organization was back on track. . . .

Teach your team the essential skills for organizing their efforts so they can achieve their targets. There are three steps to successfully organizing your workflow:

- Analyze the existing workflow
- Streamline the workflow
- Test the improvements

Analyze The Existing Workflow

To analyze the existing workflow, draw a flow chart of all activities, tasks, decision-making responsibilities, approval processes, and paperwork. Then translate it into a matrix that shows how all team members contribute to, and participate in, the workflow. These charts and matrices are enlightening; they reveal the duplication of activities, bottlenecks, and things that fall through the cracks.

The following abbreviated workflow matrix . . .

shows how Julia and her product development team analyzed their workflow. First, Julia helped her team identify their *"major tasks."* Then, each team member filled in the boxes showing their participation in the tasks.

WORKFLOW MATRIX: BEFORE STREAMLINING

MAJOR TASKS	R&D	MARKETING	SALES	OPERATIONS
1. Conduct market research		Receives requests, produces a report based on market research	May request custom research work	Provides information on production technology
2. Develop market strategy		Synthesizes research to create a conceptual plan		
3. Approve the market strategy	Approves the plan, if not, it goes back to the originator		Provides input to the plan but not approval	
4. Issue a project initiation form (PIF) **Note:** See links to other tasks	Receives the PIF's Establishes a project plan	Issues the PIF's and negotiates priorities	Participates in the negotiation of the priorities Writes copy for collateral materials	
8. Develop the marketing plan		Develops tactical plan for the concept		
9. Develop the financial budget		Participates in the budgeting process	Participates in the budgeting process	Participates in the budgeting process

Streamline The Workflow

The key to streamlining is having a solid understanding of your team's current workflow. The goal of streamlining is to use the *"as is"* information to produce a *"should be"* workflow. The better you understand the existing situation, the easier it is to make lasting changes.

Julia's team member's decided to . . .

make some changes in their workflow matrix. Julia said, *"Just make sure you think it through and that we all agree to the changes."* Julia was learning a lot from their matrices. She had never really known exactly what each employee did on a daily basis. She was usually interested in looking solely at the targets. She was now beginning to realize that her team's organization had a direct effect on their targets, especially the time to market target. She saw ways to eliminate tasks that were of no value and to simplify other approval and decision-making activities. . . .

WORKFLOW MATRIX: AFTER STREAMLINING

MAJOR TASKS	R&D	MARKETING	SALES	OPERATIONS
1. Conduct market research	Provides information on technology and participates in market research design	Receives requests, produces a report based on research, and returns it to requesters	Provides information on customer needs and participates in market research design	Provides information on production technology and participates in market research design
2. Develop and approve the product and market plan	Signs off on the plan and prepares resource plan	Synthesizes data to create a conceptual plan for the brand—for a two-year time horizon	Signs off on the plan and develops a sales approach	Provides input and must sign off on the plan
3. Issue a project initiation form (PIF)	Receives the PIF's. Tests products and conducts claims support	Issues the PIF Write claims and feasibility study	Prepares and distributes sales plan to other departments	Prepares and distributes production plan to other departments
4. Develop the financial budget	Participates in the cross-functional budgeting process	Participates in the cross-functional budgeting process	Participates in the cross-functional budgeting process	Participates in the cross-functional budgeting process

Test The Improvements

After your team streamlines its workflow, evaluate your team's performance. Did the improvements help? The key is, of course, measuring the improvements.

The following are tests or measures, of whether your improvements have been effective.

- How much has customer satisfaction increased (*number of reduced complaints per week, number of positive comments per week, etc.)*
- How much have costs of production or service decreased? *(10 percent reduced ingredient cost, 5 percent reduced delivery cost, etc.)*
- How much has workflow efficiency improved? *(20 percent less research and development time, 30 percent reduction in assembly time, etc.)*
- How much has overall quality improved? *(70 percent less defects, 20 percent less customer returns, etc.)*
- How much has employee satisfaction increased? *(25 percent less employee complaints, 50 percent reduction in turnover, etc.)*
- How much has net profit increased? *(10 percent improvement in annual ROI, forty percent reduction in uncollectable accounts receivable, etc.)*

Constantly question your team's workflow. Are there ways to further streamline it? Successful leaders know that change is not a one-time event—change is a continual process. Just because your team changed its workflow once doesn't mean that you don't need to change it again.

New problems will always arise, and technological innovations are inevitable. If you don't test improvements and continuously evaluate your workflow, your targets are in jeopardy.

> ***Julia and her team . . .***
> spent the next six months implementing their streamlined workflow. As the leader, Julia continued to work with her team so that everyone remained focused on their responsibilities. She also empowered the team members to make their own changes in the workflow. Julia pushed them to constantly search for better ways to organize their work so they could reach their targets.

Take the lead in improving your organization's workflow; *"shake it up"* so you can *"shake out"* better performance. If you don't shake up the organization, someone else, like a team member, boss, or competitor, will. An effective leader never accepts *"good enough"* or relies on a past success.

Do you remember the anecdote about the frog in a pot of boiling water? A frog thrown into a pot of boiling water will jump out immediately! The same frog placed in a pot of cool water, where the temperature slowly reaches a boil, will stay put. The moral of the story is: stay put and you'll be in trouble.

CHAPTER SEVEN WORKSHEET: ORGANIZING YOUR WORK

1. Draw a flow chart in the space provided, of all activities, tasks, decision-making responsibilities, approval processes, and paperwork.

2. Translate your flow chart into a workflow matrix that shows how all team members contribute to, and participate in, the workflow.

	Responsibility of:			
Major Tasks				
1.				
2.				
3.				
4.				
5.				
6.				
7.				
8.				
9.				
10.				

3. Examine your workflow matrix. Streamline the workflow and create a new matrix.

Note: There is a also a blank workflow matrix in the Appendix for you to photocopy and use.

	RESPONSIBILITY OF:			
MAJOR TASKS				
1.				
2.				
3.				
4.				
5.				
6.				
7.				
8.				
9.				
10.				

4. How will you test your improvements?

5. How often will you evaluate your workflow?

Promote Self-Management

People like to make their own decisions and accept responsibility for them. If you have created a vision, defined a set of values, established clear targets, and organized the workflow, then you have *"gone before"* your team and blazed the path. Now it's time to step back and *"walk behind"* your team. They have the tools necessary to assume many of the managing activities you are accustomed to handling. The more you encourage and empower your team to manage itself, the more time you will have to lead.

Why Self-Management?

When you create an environment for greater self-management, you leverage your impact as a leader. Essentially, you:

- Develop the capability to manage even more people effectively, since self-management allows you to broaden your span of influence and control
- Make yourself a valuable resource to your organization (*J.D. Rockefeller said, "I will pay more money for a person who has the skills to lead and motivate people, than for any other skill!"*) and your team can work together to manage the ends and the means of your organization. The nice part is that they can move the means to free you up.
- Encourage team learning. Teams that are responsible for managing daily operations are likely to make mistakes and experience problems. But, these are key ingredients of the learning process.

Challenges Of Self-Management

Promoting self-management is not easy. You are likely to encounter some challenges along the way. Following are several challenges you might face in promoting self-management, why they exist, and some ways to respond:

Note: For detailed tools and information on self-management, please see *Succeeding As A Self-Managed Team,* also from the Practical Guidebook Collection.

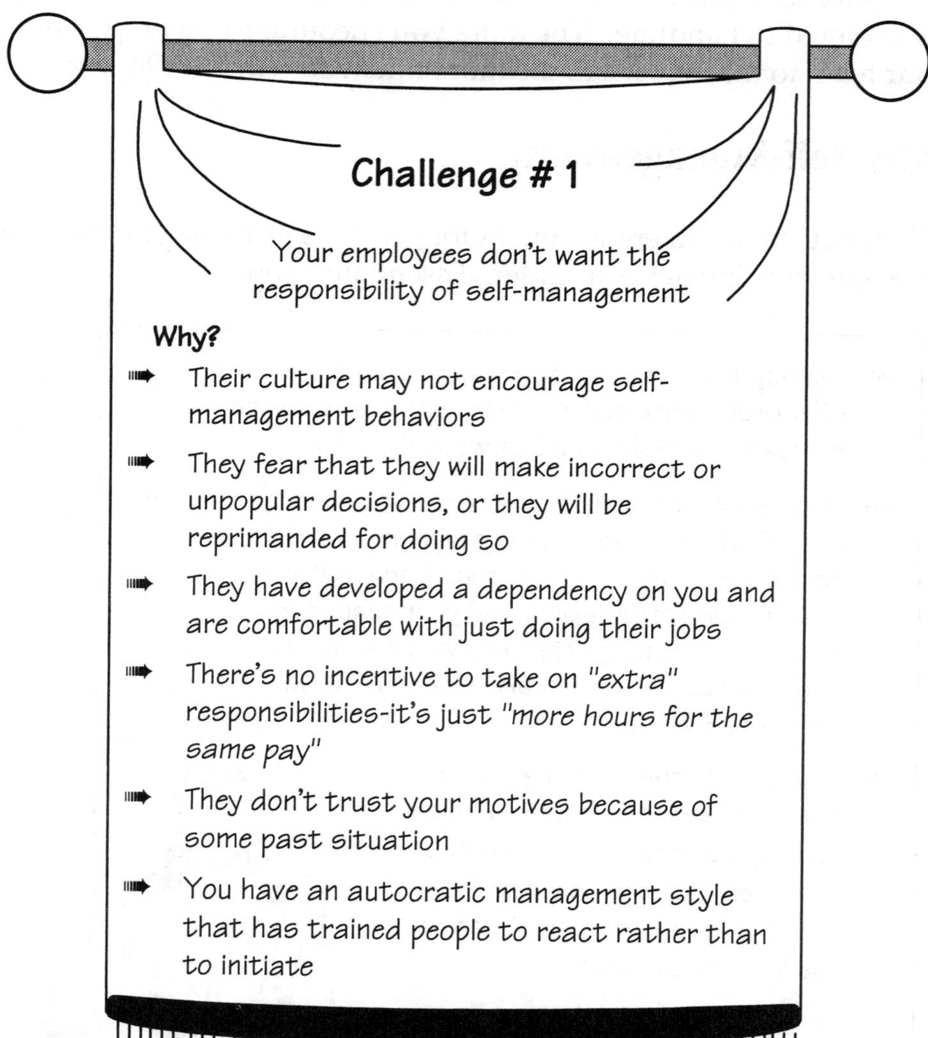

Challenge # 1
Your employees don't want the responsibility of self-management
Why?
Their culture may not encourage self-management behaviors
They fear that they will make incorrect or unpopular decisions, or they will be reprimanded for doing so
They have developed a dependency on you and are comfortable with just doing their jobs
There's no incentive to take on "extra" responsibilities-it's just "more hours for the same pay"
They don't trust your motives because of some past situation
You have an autocratic management style that has trained people to react rather than to initiate

Ways to respond:

- Have individuals determine a lead spokesperson, a peer, to help them implement self-management
- Introduce the idea of self-management on a trial basis where both you and your employees can manage problems as they arise and *"pull back"* at any time
- Assign them some of your management functions, like scheduling or interviewing, and make these functions part of their job descriptions
- Provide your employees with rewards and incentives for taking on more responsibilities
- Provide training in problem solving, how to schedule work weeks, etc.
- Refrain from providing answers to all their questions; allow them to seek their own solutions
- Change your autocratic style of management—your employees should start to take more initiative

Challenge # 2

You don't want to give up your power and responsibilities

Why?

- You are more comfortable being a "hands-on" manager because that way your employees are less likely to make a mistake
- You enjoy having all the answers because it makes you feel good
- You fear you will lose some of your power, respect, perks, or possibly your position
- You do not feel competent and trained to manage any other way, and you worry whether you can change your style and approach in mid-career
- You are concerned that the people working for you will become so good they will replace you

Ways to respond:

- ➠ Learn more about leadership to help you define a new role for yourself
- ➠ Speak with your boss on a regular basis and get his or her support for the changes you are making in your job description
- ➠ Seek out and take on other challenges in your organization
- ➠ Talk with peers who are experiencing the same challenges; they may provide some solutions
- ➠ Take a day off from work and let your employees work without you—let them develop their confidence and competence—and prove that they can manage without your direct control

Closing The Loop

Remember Jane from Chapter Three? . . .

Jane was the leader who scored a "73" on the diagnostic survey. She had low scores on Questions 17 to 20. While it was her perception that she encouraged her employees to be self-managing and to solve their own problems, her employees thought otherwise.

On the surface, it may appear that Jane is a great boss to work for. She takes care of everything. Her employees don't have to think; they rely on her to take care of all the important matters and problems. While this style may be appropriate for some employees or cultures, there are many people who are motivated by interesting or challenging work that helps them grow.

Jane's employees told her that she was controlling, and that she did not allow them to take chances or make decisions. The result was that many of the team members were becoming bored and unmotivated. Jane's employees are ready for a self-managing atmosphere and Jane is not. It's probably safe to say that Jane is worried that her people will make mistakes, so she does the important things herself. We might also guess that she enjoys having all the answers because it makes her look smart.

Jane listened to her people and decided to promote an atmosphere of self-management by doing the following:

- Going back to college to learn more about effective leadership skills. This would help her begin to understand the kinds of things she should be doing and the functions she should be delegating to others.
- Investing more time meeting and talking with other department managers. Thus creating better working relationships with her team's internal customers.

As a result, Jane learned several new approaches to promote self-management in her company:

- Focus on team goals instead of individual goals.
- Have leaders make less day-to-day decisions and more long-term decisions.
- Initiate comprehensive 360° performance evaluations.
- Implement a recognition process tied to team values.

People like to make their own decisions and accept responsibility for them. Just like Jane, many of us who aspire to be better leaders have to learn new skills and approaches to truly expand our impact.

CHAPTER EIGHT WORKSHEET: SELF-MANAGEMENT FOR YOUR TEAM

1. How ready is your team for self-management?

2. What opportunities do you have to lead your team into self-management?

3. What is your biggest challenge in promoting self-management?

4. How will you deal with this challenge?

5. What are some other challenges you will face?

6. How will you deal with them?

CHAPTER NINE

THE EVOLVING LEADERSHIP ROLE

As a leader, you are probably feeling overwhelmed by your commitments and responsibilities. Where should you invest your energy on a daily basis? What roles should you play? These are good questions. Since the goal of leadership impact is to promote self-management, a leader's primary focus should be on creating an environment in which employees manage themselves. There are four roles leaders play in supporting such an environment:

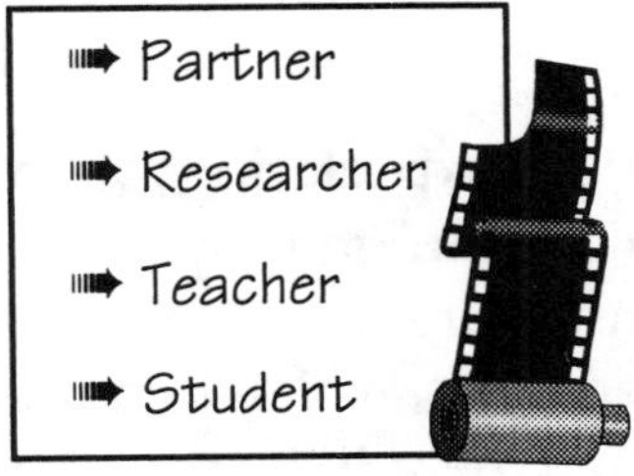

Traditional leadership models place the leader at the top as a *"Director."* Organizations are too information-rich and complex for this Director model to work effectively. The new leadership model places the leader in the center of the organization, integrated into its fabric.

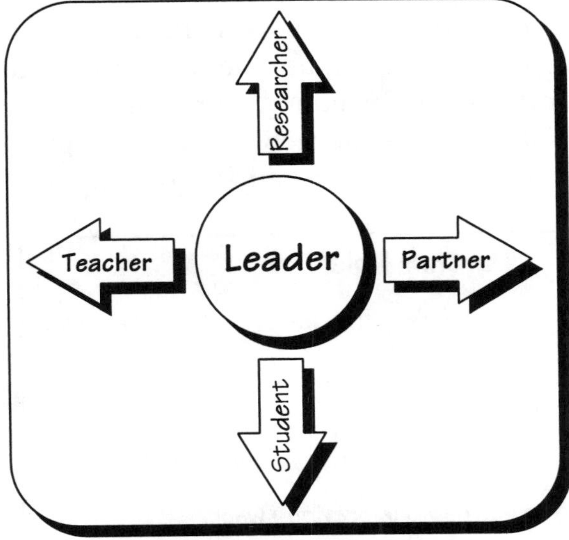

Let's take a look at the purpose, responsibilities, and associated activities for each of these roles:

Partner

Purpose

To be a partner with team members, communicating frequently and openly, so there is growth for both parties

Responsibilities

Be candid and clear about expectations with all members of your organization. Meet with your employees to discuss, formulate, negotiate, agree on, and write down these responsibilities. Teach employees how to keep a *"to do"* list to manage performance expectations. Encourage them to be direct with you in managing their *"to do"* list. Spend about 20 percent of your time doing this every week; your communication problems will disappear and the level of employee commitment will increase.

For example, one software development manager, responsible for helping her staff juggle multiple projects, built simple on-line project estimating and tracking spreadsheets for team members to list and track specific tasks. Team members can update the spreadsheet and share information on the network with each other at any time. They find it extremely useful for organizing what may appear to be conflicting and overwhelming responsibilities.

Partner Role Tips

- Stop by each employee's office to review expectations.
- Always talk about the organization's vision and the values in meetings.
- Talk with each employee about his or her *"to do"* list.
- Review lessons learned the previous week.
- Let someone else lead a problem-solving session.

Researcher

Purpose

The researcher's purpose is to seek out and use new ideas from team members, and bring in new ideas from outside the organization.

Responsibilities

As a researcher, dedicate 10 percent of your time acquiring, distributing, and assimilating new ideas, methods, technologies, and approaches that might enhance the vision, support the values, and improve your organization. Learning teams require a constant influx of new information.

For example, one new idea from an unlikely source—an employee in the Accounting Department of an organization—resulted in a $10 million product. The idea wouldn't have been discovered if a manager didn't regularly ask his employees about new uses for an existing product.

Researcher Role Tips

- Read journals related and unrelated to the industry.
- Send people to attend conferences.
- Conduct *"what's new"* and *"I wish"* sessions.
- Ask for suggestions and reward new ideas.
- Study other organizations and their methods.

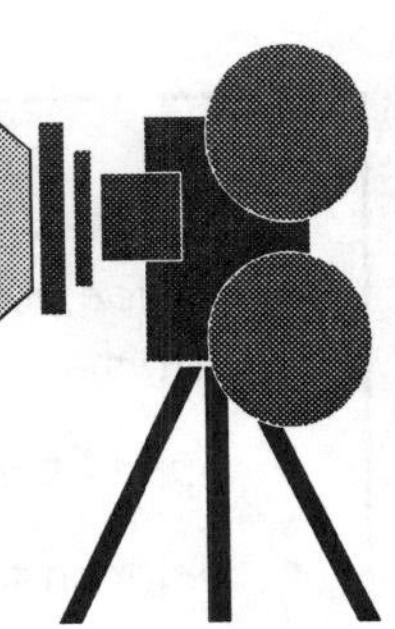

Teacher

Purpose

The teacher's purpose is to develop your employees' abilities to think on their own, exercise common sense, and ask the right questions.

Responsibilities

Any learning organization needs teachers. Thirty percent of your time should be dedicated to teaching your team members how to solve problems, how to make decisions, and how to uphold your organization's values. Refrain from doing all the work; teach your people to do your job. Then you will have the time to be a leader. Discuss your decision-making process with others. Involve your employees in structured problem-solving sessions.

For example, in one particularly changeable organization, a production manager chose to dedicate one full day per week to *"change management"* techniques and applications. Team morale improved immediately, weekly production rose 10 percent in a month's time, and resistance to new ideas dropped dramatically.

Teacher Role Tips

- Praise people's decisions and problem-solving efforts.
- Spend time offering constructive criticism.
- Be open to constructive criticism about yourself and your work.

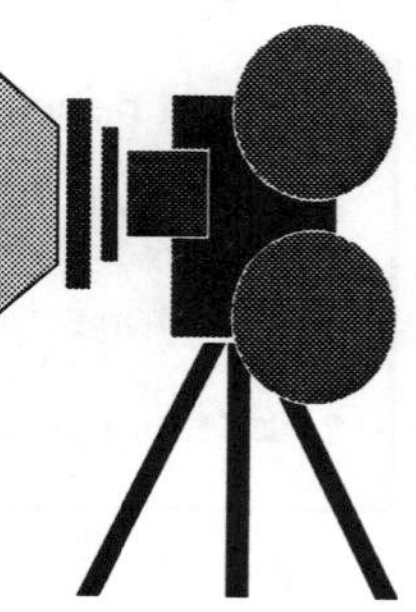

Student

Purpose

The student's purpose is to understand what each employee confronts in his or her job.

Responsibilities

Many leaders have a tendency to see complex problems as simple ones. They are often too far removed from the *"real"* workflow to see the innate complexities and frustrations experienced by employees. As a result, they frustrate employees by offering simplistic and irrelevant solutions. Before you offer the simple and obvious solutions, understand the complexities underlying the problems your employees are facing. Spend at least 10 percent of your time understanding what your people do and how your systems function.

For example, one large mortgage banking organization, heeding the advice of a training consulting firm over the objections of its managers, elected to send all managers through the same software skills training as line employees, even though the managers wouldn't be using the software. Once the software was implemented, both managers and employees found that communication between them had greatly improved, and day-to-day work problems were easier to solve.

Student Role Tips

- Do another employee's job to get an appreciation of the workflow.
- Let someone else do your job so they have an appreciation of it.
- Eliminate non value-added activities and slay "sacred cows."
- Staple yourself to a customer purchase order and follow it as it weaves its way through your organization. *(Thus, you will learn who takes the order, what gets done with it, when the critical stages occur, hold-ups etc.)*

CHAPTER TEN

SUMMARY

Vision, values, targets, and workflow are the critical elements of effective leadership. There are some specific steps you can take to acquire these skills. Use the leadership model provided in this book as a map to guide you through these steps; it's an extremely effective, adaptable model.

It will help you focus on the two fundamentals of leadership impact: managing both the ends and the means, and building a learning team.

If you are doubtful whether you can develop your leadership impact, don't be. You *can* do it! The following story might give you the confidence to implement what you've learned.

Several years ago, fifteen hikers were saved because they had a map. Lost in a mountain pass in the dead of winter, with little survival gear or time before the elements would overwhelm them, they used the one map they had to plan their route to civilization and safety. With their map, they identified their location, found a village, and began to hike out. Thirty-six hours later, the group stumbled into the village barely alive. They discovered, however, that the name of the town they were in was not the name of the town on the map. Even more surprising, they discovered that the map they had used was a map of the Pyrenees in Spain. They were lost in the Alps in Switzerland. *(The map had led them to follow a small valley to a larger one, and since mountain villages are usually situated in valleys, the logic worked.)*

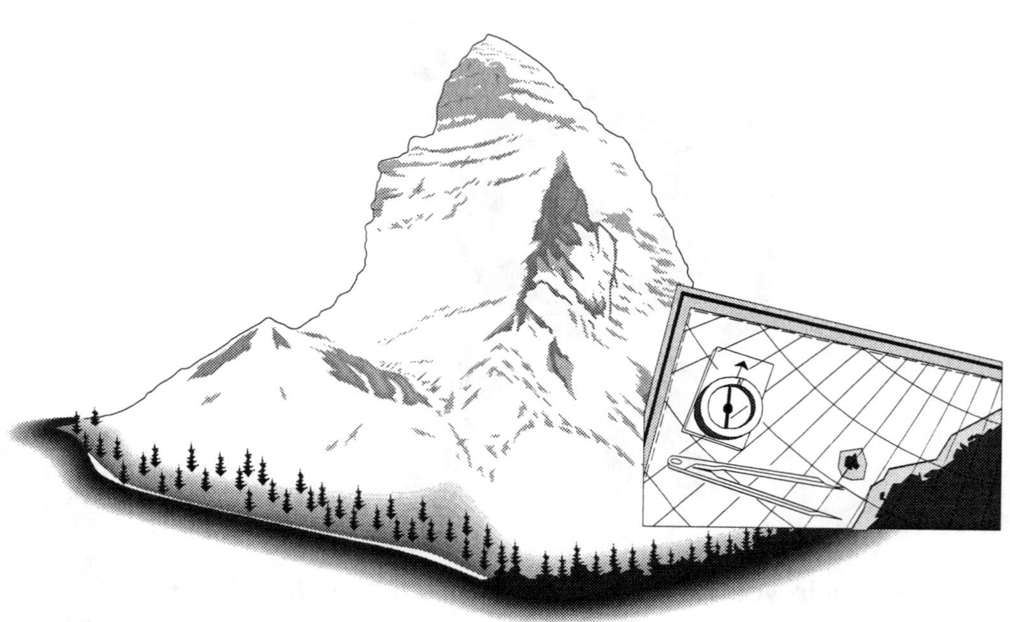

It's really better to have some kind of map than none at all. But think of all you can do when you have the *"right"* map, such as this guidebook!

The four roles of Partner, Researcher, Teacher, and Student will help you understand where to invest your energy as a leader. However, this doesn't mean that you have to adopt every point tomorrow. Instead, begin an evolution of incorporating one or two of these activities every month, and delegating less valued activities to other team members. By doing this, you'll eventually become a partner, a researcher, a teacher, and a student.

Leadership is changing. As a leader, you have to know when to go before, and when to walk behind your team. If this guidebook has changed your thinking even a little bit, it was worth reading. A door in you has probably been nudged open. Keep it open by coming back to this book from time to time. There will be something new for you to learn each time, because you will be different every time you read it.

Reference Materials And Reproducible Forms

TEAM SITUATION SURVEY

Respond to the following statements by circling the appropriate number on a scale of 1 to 5. Your honest responses are important to your team's performance.

1	3	5
Strongly disagree	Neither agree nor disagree	Strongly agree

1.	I have a clear vision of what our team is working towards.	**1 2 3 4 5**
2.	This vision provides a sense of purpose.	**1 2 3 4 5**
3.	The vision is *"motivating."*	**1 2 3 4 5**
4.	I think the vision is the *"right"* vision.	**1 2 3 4 5**
	Subtotal	
5.	I have a clear understanding of our team's *"ground rules."*	**1 2 3 4 5**
6.	These rules are important.	**1 2 3 4 5**
7.	I follow these rules.	**1 2 3 4 5**
8.	The rules are appropriate for every member of our team.	**1 2 3 4 5**
	Subtotal	
9.	The existing team is effective.	**1 2 3 4 5**
10.	Our team's organization is consistent with the vision.	**1 2 3 4 5**
11.	Our team's organization facilitates communication.	**1 2 3 4 5**
12.	Employees can change the workflow as needed.	**1 2 3 4 5**
	Subtotal	
13.	Our team has clearly defined targets.	**1 2 3 4 5**
14.	The targets are reasonable.	**1 2 3 4 5**
15.	The targets are consistent with the vision.	**1 2 3 4 5**
16.	Mistakes are treated as learning opportunities.	**1 2 3 4 5**
	Subtotal	
17.	Leader allows employees to be self-managing.	**1 2 3 4 5**
18.	Employees are encouraged to solve problems.	**1 2 3 4 5**
19.	Leader provides constructive feedback.	**1 2 3 4 5**
20.	Leader rewards performance.	**1 2 3 4 5**
	Total	

Vision And Targets Matrix

	Product/Service Targets			
Elements of our vision	**Target # 1**	**Target # 2**	**Target # 3**	**Target # 4**

●= Strong impact ◒= Medium impact O= Little impact

Workflow Matrix

Major Tasks	Responsibility of:			
1.				
2.				
3.				
4.				
5.				
6.				
7.				
8.				
9.				
10.				

Assessing Selected Leadership Competencies

This survey is designed to give you a better understanding of the some of the skills and competencies required of successful leaders. The following instructions explain how to evaluate your ability and how to rate how important each competency is to your complete role.

Column A: Competencies

Column A identifies 45 selected competencies critical to effective leadership. *After reviewing all items,* complete columns B and C

Column B: Evaluate Your Ability

Using the rating scale below, rate your abilities and write the results in Column B next to each item:

10 = Outstanding ability *("one of my outstanding talents")*
7 = Above average ability *("compared to my ability in other areas")*
5 = Average or moderate ability
3 = Below average ability
0 = No experience or training in this area

Column C: Describe Your Job or Position

Use the rating scale below to reflect how important each item in the survey is to your job. Record these ratings in Column C.

10 = Outstanding ability *("one of my outstanding talents")*
7 = Above average ability *("compared to my ability in other areas")*
5 = Average or moderate ability
3 = Below average ability
0 = No experience or training in this area

Be Discriminating!

Force yourself to distribute your ratings this way:

3 to 8 *"10's,"* 6 to 12 *"7's,"* 10 to 25 *"5's,"* 6 to 12 *"3's,"* and as many *"0's"* as appropriate. Your results will be more accurate.

Column D: Identify Your Strengths And Development Needs

Then use Column D as described later on.

A COMPETENCIES	B YOUR ABILITY	C IMPORTANCE ON JOB	D STRENGTHS AND NEEDS
1. Knowing how others acquire and use knowledge, skills, attitudes; understanding individual differences in learning.			
2. Understanding and/or using computer applications.			
3. Preparing clear business plans and project statements which describe desired outputs.			
4. Describing and tracking team behaviors and their efforts.			
5. Knowing the purpose and processes of each function or discipline being addressed.			
6. Selecting, developing, and using management methodologies such as statistical and data collection techniques for formal inquiry.			
7. Knowing how the functions of a business work and are related to each other; knowing the economic impact of business decisions.			
8. Assessing project alternatives in terms of their financial, psychological, and strategic advantages and disadvantages.			
9. Knowing the elements that define an industry or sector, such as critical issues, economic vulnerabilities, measurements, distribution channels, inputs, outputs, and information sources.			
10. Seeing various teams as dynamic, political, economic, and social systems which have multiple goals; using this larger perspective as a framework for understanding and influencing events and change.			
11. Knowing the techniques and approaches used in project management; understanding their appropriate use.			
12. Knowing the strategy, structure, power networks, financial position, and systems of your organization.			
13. Planning, organizing, and monitoring work which may be occurring in parallel.			
14. Storing massive amounts of data in an easily retrievable form.			
15. Helping team members recognize and understand their personal needs, values, problems, alternatives, and goals as related to your project.			
16. Communicating information, opinions, observations, and conclusions so that they are easily understood and can be acted upon.			
17. Influencing groups so that tasks, relationships, and individual needs are addressed.			

A Competencies	B Your Ability	C Importance On Job	D Strengths And Needs
18. Securing win-win agreements while successfully representing a special interest in a decision.			
19. Presenting information verbally so that an intended purpose is clearly achieved.			
20. Gathering information for stimulating insights in customers and other individuals and groups through use of interviews, questionnaires, and other probing methods.			
21. Establishing relationships and networks across a broad range of people and groups.			
22. Preparing written materials that follow generally accepted rules of style and form, are appropriate for the audience, are creative, and accomplish their intended purpose.			
23. Analyzing, synthesizing, and drawing conclusions from complex sales data.			
24. Gathering information from printed and other recorded sources; identifying and using information specialists and reference services and aids.			
25. Recognizing, exploring, and using a broad range of ideas and practices; thinking logically and creatively without undue influence from personal biases.			
26. Conceptualizing and developing theoretical and practical frameworks that describe complex ideas in understandable and practical ways.			
27. Objectively recognizing and analyzing what is happening in or across project situations.			
28. Knowing one's personal values, needs, interests, styles, and competencies, and their effect(s) on others.			
29. Projecting trends, and visualizing possible and probable futures and their implications.			
30. Being aware of the ethical choices which need to be made when faced with difficult, conflicting options.			
31. Monitoring one's own emotional responses to differing situations, people, and patterns which may lead to inflexible behavior.			
32. Listening actively to the content, process signals, and cues for purposes of diagnosing underlying feelings and motivations.			
33. Exchanging feedback in timely and constructive ways to build open, collaborative relationships.			
34. Balancing support and challenge in relationships, influencing and gaining commitment, and remaining open to influence from others.			

A COMPETENCIES	B YOUR ABILITY	C IMPORTANCE ON JOB	D STRENGTHS AND NEEDS
35. Handling conflict by challenging without alienating, and having the courage to confront potentially difficult interpersonal areas.			
36. Acknowledging personal and professional limits through a willingness to ask for help.			
37. Living with ambiguous, uncertain, and complex situations without undue stress.			
38. Facilitating the setting of short- and medium-term goals in light of longer-term missions or purposes.			
39. Understanding the nature of change and the change process, including why people and *"larger systems"* resist changes.			
40. Facilitating change efforts to encourage widespread participation in the design and implementation of change.			
41. Creating working contracts by clarifying mutual expectations and renegotiating the terms of work when necessary.			
42. Choosing appropriate methods for data collection while encouraging *"customer"* ownership of data.			
43. Selecting from a range of models for understanding and diagnosing project problems with individuals, groups, or organizations.			
44. Designing interventions creatively and purposefully and being able to redesign project systems, schedules, and processes on the spot.			
45. Disengaging well from *"pressure-filled"* assignments and learning from each project.			
46.			
47.			
48.			
49.			
50.			

Column D: Identifying Strengths and Development Areas

Strengths: To identify your key competencies, review your ratings of yourself in Column B. Put a "+" in Column D next to those items where you rated yourself *"10."* Knowledge of your abilities is particularly helpful if it leads to actions to further develop the competencies or to find ways to use them most effectively. List below three strengths you feel would be most useful to further capitalize on:

ITEM #	BRIEF DESCRIPTION OF STRENGTH	HOW TO CAPITALIZE ON STRENGTH
1.		
2.		
3.		

Development Areas: To identify your leadership development areas, subtract your rating of importance *(Column C)* from your rating of your abilities *(Column B)*. Put the answer in Column D. Include the minus sign if it is a negative number. For example, if you rated your ability as a *"3,"* and the importance a *"10,"* you would put *"-7"* in Column D. The larger the negative number, the greater the need for improvement. Every negative number in Column D indicates some need for improvement. List below three (3) development areas you most want to work on, and your plans to develop this area of needed improvement.

ITEM #	DEVELOPMENT AREA	DEVELOPMENT PLAN
1.		
2.		
3.		

The Practical Guidebook Collection

Quality Improvement Series

- Meetings That Work!
- Continuous Improvement Tools Volume 1
- Continuous Improvement Tools Volume 2
- Step-By-Step Problem Solving
- Satisfying Internal Customers First!
- Continuous Process Improvement
- Improving Through Benchmarking
- Succeeding As A Self-Managed Team
- Reengineering In Action

Management Skills Series

- Coaching Through Effective Feedback
- Expanding Leadership Impact
- Mastering Change Management
- Effective Induction And Training
- Re-Creating Teams During Transitions

High Performance Team Series

- Success Through Teamwork
- Team Decision-Making Techniques
- Measuring Team Performance
- Building A Dynamic Team

High-Impact Training Series

- Creating High-Impact Training
- Identifying Targeted Training Needs
- Mapping A Winning Training Approach
- Producing High-Impact Learning Tools
- Applying Successful Training Techniques
- Measuring The Impact Of Training
- Make Your Training Results Last

EVALUATION AND FEEDBACK FORM

We need your help to continuously improve the quality of the resources provided through the Richard Chang Associates, Inc., Publications Division. We would greatly appreciate your input and suggestions regarding this particular guidebook, as well as future guidebook interests.

Please photocopy this form before completing it, since other readers may use this guidebook. Thank you in advance for your feedback.

Guidebook Title: ______________________________

1. Overall, how would you rate your *level of satisfaction* with this guidebook? Please circle your response.

Extremely Dissatisfied		Satisfied		Extremely Satisfied
1	2	3	4	5

2. What specific *concepts or methods* did you find most helpful?

____

____

3. What specific *concepts or methods* did you find least helpful?

____

____

4. As an individual who may purchase additional guidebooks in the future, what *characteristics/features/benefits* are most important to you in making a decision to purchase a guidebook *(or another similar book)*?

____

____

5. What additional *subject matter/topic areas* would you like to see addressed in future guidebooks?

____

____

Name *(optional)*:

Address: ______________________________

C/S/Z: ____________________ **Phone** (   ) ____________________

PLEASE FAX YOUR RESPONSES TO: (714) 756-0853 USA
OR (0171) 837-6348 UK